This Book Donated to
the Children of Placerville by
Mr. Gordon Purdy
Who Loved Children and
Books in That Order -
Usually.

GEORGE ARMSTRONG CUSTER

GENERAL OF THE U.S. CAVALRY

THEODORE LINK

rosen central
Primary Source™

The Rosen Publishing Group, Inc., New York

Published in 2004 by The Rosen Publishing Group, Inc.
29 East 21st Street, New York, NY 10010

First Edition

Library of Congress Cataloging-in-Publication Data

Link, Theodore.
George Armstrong Custer / by Theodore Link.— 1st ed.
    v. cm. — (Primary sources of famous people in American history)
Summary: A biography of the Civil War general known for his part in the disastrous battle at the Little Bighorn in 1876.
Includes bibliographical references (p.) and index.
Contents: Autie — The Civil War — Going West — Chief Sitting Bull and Little Bighorn — Custer's last stand.
ISBN 0-8239-4110-8 (lib. bdg.)
ISBN 0-8239-4182-5 (pbk.)
6-pack ISBN 0-8239-4309-7
1. Custer, George Armstrong, 1839–1876—Juvenile literature. 2. Generals—United States—Biography—Juvenile literature. 3. United States. Army—Biography—Juvenile literature. 4. United States—History—Civil War, 1861–1865—Biography—Juvenile literature. 5. Indians of North America—Wars—Great Plains—Juvenile literature. 6. Little Bighorn, Battle of the, Mont., 1876—Juvenile literature. 7. Little Bighorn, Battle of the, Mont., 1876. [1. Custer, George Armstrong, 1839–1876. 2. Generals.]
I. Title. II. Series.
E467.1.C99L56 2003
973.8'2'092—dc21
                                                     2003003801

Manufactured in the United States of America

Photo credits: cover National Archives and Records Administration; pp. 5, 7 National Portrait Gallery, Smithsonian Institute/Art Resource, NY; pp. 6, 8, 18, 22, 27, 28, 29 (bottom) © North Wind Picture Archives; pp. 9, 12 Library of Congress Prints and Photographs Division; p. 11 © Medford Historical Society Collection/Corbis; p. 13 © Bettmann/Corbis; p. 14 Joslyn Art Museum, Omaha, Nebraska; pp. 15 (X-33621), 16 (B-697), 21 (X-31704), 29 (top) (X-31275) Denver Public Library, Western History Collection; pp. 17, 24 © Corbis; p. 19 © Hulton/Archive/Getty Images; pp. 23, 25 Western History Collection, University of Oklahoma; p. 26 The Stapleton Collection/The Bridgeman Art Library.

CONTENTS

AUTIE

In his short life, George Armstrong Custer became a famous leader. He became a legend after his stunning death at the Little Bighorn.

He was born on December 5, 1839, in New Rumley, Ohio. His family called him "Armstrong." He could not say his name. He called himself "Autie." The name stuck.

ONE BIG FAMILY

Autie had seven brothers and sisters. Four were older and three were younger.

George "Autie" Custer was photographed as a cadet at West Point around 1860. He poses with a Colt-Root pocket revolver.

Autie and his father loved jokes. No one in the family was safe from their pranks.

Autie went to West Point to become a soldier. He had trouble following rules. He made his friends laugh at the wrong times. Autie got into a lot of trouble. But his classmates made him a leader.

Custer finished last in his class at West Point!

George Armstrong Custer had become a brigadier general when this picture was made in 1863. He is wearing a velvet jacket with gold braid and stars.

2 THE CIVIL WAR

"Autie" Custer graduated from West Point in 1861. The Civil War had begun. The South had broken away from the United States.

Custer wanted to help the country stay whole. He joined the cavalry, gathering news about the enemy. Very good at his job, he quickly moved up in rank. In 1863, Custer became the youngest general in the army!

At West Point, students learn to use the newest weapons and ways to fight wars.

HARPER'S WEEKLY.

A JOURNAL OF CIVILIZATION.

VOL. VIII.—No. 377.]   NEW YORK, SATURDAY, MARCH 19, 1864.   [$4.00 FOR FOUR MONTHS.
[$3.00 PER YEAR IN ADVANCE.

Entered according to Act of Congress, in the Year 1864, by Harper & Brothers, in the Clerk's Office of the District Court for the Southern District of New York.

George Armstrong Custer became a Civil War hero. He is pictured here on the cover of *Harper's Weekly* in 1864.

His job was to lead a Michigan cavalry group. The soldiers were very loyal to him. Custer had his own personal flag. It helped his men find him in battle. He became one of the best leaders of either side.

By the war's end in 1865, Custer was famous. He had helped the North beat the South. To people in the North, he was a hero.

CUSTER'S SWEETHEART

Custer had a childhood sweetheart named Elizabeth Bacon. He called her "Libbie." They married in 1864.

This portrait of Custer and his wife, Libbie, was taken by the famous photographer Mathew Brady sometime between 1860 and 1864.

After the war, Custer became a lieutenant colonel in the Seventh Cavalry. The cavalry's job was to help keep peace in the South.

The army sent the Seventh Cavalry to the West in 1867. People were settling there. The American government encouraged people to live in the West.

General Custer, Libbie Custer, and Custer's brother Thomas *(standing).* Thomas Custer also died in 1876 at the Battle of the Little Bighorn.

Lieutenant Colonel George Custer was photographed with Indian scouts and his dogs.

13

But the Indians had lived there for a long time. The tribes were angry. Some declared war on the settlers. Custer's cavalry worked to protect the settlers.

In 1868, Custer led his men against the Cheyenne Indians. Custer's men beat them at the Washita River. Most of the tribe gave up. Custer was a hero again.

Many Indian tribes lived on the plains. They lived in tepees. This picture shows a Sioux camp.

THE PLATTE RIVER AT NORTH PLATTE.—SKETCHED AT T. R. DAVIS.—[SEE FIRST PAGE.]

ETHAN ALLEN.

We give on page 485 a handsome engraving of the fast trotter, Ethan Allen. The original of this picture was taken by instantaneous photography by Rockwood, and is as perfect a picture of the animal as can be obtained.

Prominent as Ethan Allen is in the Racing Calendar, it is almost impossible to give the truth in regard to his pedigree and performances. He is now a little over 18 years of age, having been foaled in Hague, Warren County, New York, on June 19, 1849. He was bred by Mr. O. S. Roe, who formerly owned him, and from whom we have obtained the few reliable statements which are to be had regarding his pedigree. His sire was Vermont Black Hawk, and his dam a gray mare whose pedigree is unknown, and who was brought to New York a short time before the birth of Ethan Allen. He is supposed to be a descendant on the mother's side of Messenger, but this is not positively known, although it is frequently very positively stated.

Of his performances previous to the fast race made by him on June 21, 1867, we know little that is positive. He was beaten by Flora Temple at Baltimore, December 1, 1850, in 2.25½; again at Fashion Course during the same season in 2.25; and beat Columbus, Jun., at the National Horse Fair, Boston, in 1850, in 2.31.

His most remarkable trot was made on Fashion Course, Long Island, on June 21, 18 where he and his running mate beat the fam Dexter in harness in the remarkable time 2.15, 2.16, and 2.19. The horses were in sp did condition at the time, and the day and t were particularly fine, but no one expected any thing like the extraordinary speed displ by both animals would be exhibited. The h has never been beaten in this country.

TRAVELING ON A PRAIRIE CANON.—[SEE FIRST PAGE.]

GENERAL CUSTER'S INTERVIEW WITH PAWNEE KILLER.—[SEE FIRST PAGE.]

Four drawings from an 1867 *Harper's Weekly* portray Custer with Sioux Indians.

15

Custer was a great hunter. Many people wanted to hunt with him. Custer once took a Russian duke with him when he went hunting! They became good friends.

In 1872, General George A. Custer *(left)* and Grand Duke Alexis of Russia posed in a studio wearing their hunting clothes.

General Custer and others with a grizzly bear they killed on a hunt in 1874. They are in the Black Hills of South Dakota.

17

4 CHIEF SITTING BULL AND THE LITTLE BIGHORN

In 1873, Custer led his men into the Dakota Territory. They blazed a trail through the wilderness. The Northern Pacific Railroad laid its tracks along this path. Custer enjoyed the trip. He got to show off as a hunter and a woodsman.

The Indians tried hard to chase the railway off of Indian land. Custer's men protected the workers who were laying tracks for the Northern Pacific Railway.

When the railroads reached across the West, it became easier for white people to settle on Indian lands. These railroad workers were photographed in 1885.

19

In 1874, miners found gold in the Dakota Territory. Many people moved there to get rich.

The Sioux Indians owned the land. They did not want settlers to take it. They declared war. Chief Sitting Bull brought many of the Sioux tribes together for the fight.

DID YOU KNOW?

Custer wrote stories about his adventures. In 1874, they were printed in a book called *My Life on the Plains*.

Custer led a large expedition of men, horses, and wagons across the plains in 1874. Many of the men wore military uniforms.

By 1876, the United States wanted to force Indians onto reservations. Custer was ordered to drive the tribes off of their land. Custer had to find Sitting Bull and his warriors.

The Sioux were gathered near the Little Bighorn River. The Seventh Cavalry got ready for battle.

The Battle of the Little Bighorn took place in these hills. This is how the land looks today.

Sitting Bull is shown here on Indian land in the Dakota Territory. Custer's mission was to drive the Sioux Indians off their land.

CUSTER'S LAST STAND

Custer attacked the Indians on June 25, 1876. He and 210 horsemen charged through a pass at the Little Bighorn. Another group of his men attacked the Indian camp from the side. Other soldiers circled around to do the same.

Sitting Bull's men drove away the first group. Custer and his soldiers reached the battlefield too late to help them.

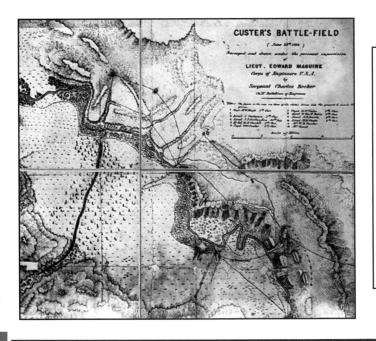

The army studied this map of the battlefield after the battle. The army wanted to learn why Custer and his men had all been killed.

Sitting Bull wears an impressive headdress. He was a Sioux chief who refused to sign a land treaty with the American government. As a result, white people were afraid of him.

25

The Indian warriors wiped them out. Custer died with his men. Sitting Bull had won the battle.

Two days later, other soldiers found Custer's body on the battlefield. They named the spot Custer Hill. He had fought there until the end.

Amos Bad Heart Buffalo drew this picture of the Battle of the Little Bighorn in the Montana Territory. He called it *The End of the Battle.*

No one knows exactly when Custer died during his last battle. But some people think he survived until the very end.

News of the battle spread. Many people were shocked by Custer's death. Many people mourned.

Custer was only thirty-five years old when he died. He was a famous leader. People wonder what he might have done if he had lived longer.

Custer's Indian scout Curley, shown here, warned him about the size of the Indian forces at the Little Bighorn. The only survivors were Curley and Custer's horse.

Above: Four Crow Indians, who had been scouts for Custer, stand at grave markers on the site of the Battle of the Little Bighorn. Below: Here are the gravestones of Custer and his men as they look today.

TIMELINE

December 5, 1839—
George Armstrong
"Autie" Custer is born.

1857—Custer becomes
a cadet at West Point.

1861—Custer graduates
from West Point and
joins the cavalry to fight
for the Union army
during the Civil War.

1863—Custer
becomes a general in
the Union army.

1864—Custer
marries Elizabeth
"Libbie" Bacon.

1867—The army sends
Custer and the Seventh
Cavalry west to protect
settlers from angry
Native Americans.
Custer is removed from
command until 1868
for visiting Libbie
without permission.

1873—Custer and the
Seventh Cavalry go to
the Dakota Territory to
blaze a trail for the
Northern Pacific
Railroad.

June 25, 1876—Custer
and 210 of his men
die at the Battle of the
Little Bighorn.

GLOSSARY

cavalry (KA-vul-ree) A group of soldiers who ride horses into battle.

general (JEN-rul) The person in charge of leading; the army's highest rank.

lieutenant colonel (loo-TEH-nent KER-nul) The rank in the army just below a full colonel.

officer (AH-fih-sur) A leader in the army.

rank (RANK) A soldier's level of authority in the army. For example, a general is a high rank.

regiment (REH-jih-ment) A group in the military; a large group of soldiers led by a colonel.

reservation (reh-zer-VAY-shun) An area of land set aside by the government for a special purpose.

West Point (WEST POYNT) A United States military academy.

WEB SITES

Due to the changing nature of Internet links, the Rosen Publishing Group, Inc., has developed an online list of Web sites related to the subject of this book. This site is updated regularly. Please use this link to access the list:

http://www.rosenlinks.com/fpah/gacu

PRIMARY SOURCE IMAGE LIST

Page 5: George Armstrong Custer, Ambrotype, circa 1860, National Portrait Gallery, Smithsonian Institution, Washington, D.C.

Page 6: *Cadets at West Point*, hand-colord woodcut, 1850s, © North Wind Pictures.

Page 7: George Armstrong Custer, Ambrotype, circa 1863, National Portrait Gallery, Smithsonian Institution, Washington, D.C.

Page 8: *Artillery Practice, U.S. Military Academy at West Point*, hand-colored woodcut, 1850s, © North Wind Pictures.

Page 9: *Brigadier-General George A. Custer*, wood engraving after photograph by Mathew Brady, March 19, 1864, *Harper's Weekly*.

Page 11: George Armstrong Custer and wife, photograph by Mathew Brady Studio, circa 1860–1865, Still Picture Branch, National Archives.

Page 12: George Armstrong Custer, in uniform, seated with his wife and his brother Thomas W. Custer, standing, photographic print, created between 1861 and 1876.

Page 13: *Lieutenant Colonel George Custer and Scout Members*, photograph, circa 1870, courtesy Bettmann/Corbis.

Page 14: *Sioux Camp,* painting by Karl Bodmer, circa 1830, watercolor on paper, Joslyn Art Museum, Omaha, Nebraska.

Page 15: *Custer Expedition*, engravings by T. R. Davis, August 3, 1867, *Harper's Weekly*, from the collection of the Denver Public Library.

Page 16: General George A. Custer and Grand Duke Alexis in hunting clothes, glass plate photograph by D. F. Barry, 1872, from the collection of the Denver Public Library.

Page 17: *General Custer with Dead Grizzly Bear*, photograph by W. H. Illingworth, circa 1874, courtesy Corbis.

Page 19: Members of a Northern Pacific Railroad crew, circa 1885, courtesy Hulton/Getty/Archive Photos.

Page 21: *Custer's Expedition on the Plains*, one half of stereograph, photograph by W. H. Illingworth, 1874, from the collection of the Denver Public Library.

Page 23: *Sitting Bull*, photograph by Randall, Campbell Collection.

Page 24: "Custer's Battle-field" map, drawn by Sergeant Charles Becker, U.S. Corps of Engineers, for Reno Court of Inquiry, July 25–26, 1876. Corbis.

Page 25: *Sitting Bull in Head Dress*, photograph Campbell Collection.

Page 26: *The End of the Battle*, ink drawing on paper by Amos Bad Heart Buffalo (1869–1913), courtesy of the Stapleton Collection.

Page 29 (top): *Custer's Scouts at Battlefield, Crow*, photographed between 1880 and 1900, from the collection of the Denver Public Library.

INDEX

ABOUT THE AUTHOR

Theodore Link is an author living in Chicago.